living the borrowed life

BOOKS BY ROBERT BONAZZI

POETRY

Living the Borrowed Life (New Rivers Press 1974)

Domingo (Bilingual Cycle with C.W. Truesdale and Carlos Isla. Translated by Millie Vazquez McDaniel and Linda Scheer. Latitudes Press 1974)

ANTHOLOGIES (Editor)

Extreme Unctions and Other Last Rites, Volume I, New Departures in Fiction (Latitudes Press 1974)

Survivors of the Invention (New Poets. Latitudes 1974)

Toward Winter: Poems for the Last Decade. (Enlarged second edition, Latitudes/New Rivers 1972; first edition with H.C. Nash, Latitudes 1968)

living the borrowed life

robert bonazzi

new rivers press 1974

Poems & Drawings © 1974 by Robert Bonazzi
Library of Congress Catalog Card Number 74-20131
ISBN 0-912284-60-9   (paper)
      0-912284-61-7   (cloth)

Forty-one of these poems appeared in the magazines
Chelsea, El Corno Emplumado, Crazy Horse, Descant,
goodly company, Hearse, El Heraldo, Latitudes,
Minnesota Review, Monks Pond, New Orleans Review,
New York Times, Pan American Review, Quixote, Road
Apple Review, Salt Creek Reader, Sumac, Yes, and in
the anthologies, *The New Breed* (Prickly Pear 1974),
The Sensuous President (New Rivers 1972), *Meby In
His Carriage* (Summit 1968) and in two editions of
Toward Winter (Latitudes 1968; Latitudes/New Rivers
1972). All poems have been revised from earlier pub-
lished versions, and some have acquired new titles.
Thanks are due to the editors for reprint permission.

New Rivers Press Books are distributed by
                Serendipity Books
                1790 Shattuck Avenue
                Berkeley, California 94709

This book was manufactured in the United States
of America for New Rivers Press, P.O. Box 578,
Cathedral Station, New York, New York 10025 in
a first edition of 800 copies of which 500 have
been bound in paper and 300 in cloth, 15 of which
have been signed and numbered by the author.

FOR ROCHELLE

Contents

IV

V

VI

I

Everything intercepts us from ourselves.

—Emerson

TRAILING A FOX

Fresh tracks
      almost casual
an exercise of language in the snow

Trees are nothing
but their own identity
      last leaves complacent
wind has its own way

I follow him up the ridge
a little to the left

         *

Impossible to feel wizened
against this cliff
      I lose years down here
and the fox
      or the fox loses me

         *

I stop to mold a snowball
as small as my ambition

This is the stranger I can never throw

THE FIRST DAY OF WINTER

I walk a long way to meet
the lowest angle of light

The first day of winter
is the shortest of the year

*

Back home
I watch my cat stalk
his shadow

I can only stare

I want to know how long it takes
to feel
    for the first time
without self-importance

*

I make no relative statements

The shortest day of the year
has the longest night

SEAGULL OVER PROSPECT PARK

Dry and flat is the sound
of this gull's first flapping
    a lost hand
dropped from the sky's applause

Over the closed eye
of the water
    wings circle
out of rhythm
patience is too far inland

Circling
    he drops
feathers
    as lures for the wind

His shadow is a layer on the ice

THE INCOMPATIBLE SELF

1

In my ignorance I cross
recross firm ground

under me earth moves
as the sea moves
but with more patience

2

Paralyzed heart throws up
this same old story: I'm Jupiter
in a vacuum of minor moons

They are all children
I'm never young

3

The fear of my father dying
the fear that he might outlive me

4

Bones of dream
walk with the body in its coma

CHILDHOOD WAS NEVER A LASTING WAY OF LIFE

I waited around for adulthood
that next out-of-town bus to grab
I hoped it would change me
or change itself
when it was time

I should've known they'd be right
to sit in circles
of coffeecups & cards
Oh I fit
      finally
but that's not what I'd meant by change

*

Perhaps Aquinas *did* levitate
that's just never been enough
And Hume had these boxes
I couldn't get into

Eventually I lost Christ
in Bach's fugues

*

Ever notice how adults can cock
the thickest wristbones
in the most fragile way?
Then they stir their coffee so quietly
you'd think they'd already evolved
beyond spoons

SIMPLE POEM

How can I know if I need to cry
When does it happen
Who tells me

I've seen my mother cry
I've seen my sister cry
I've seen my brother cry

How is crying done
How have I avoided it

Who is supposed to know
(I don't know)
Who can I tell
(I can't tell)
When was the last time I cried
I've seen my father cry

DAN'S DREAM

Near the top
we toss away useless provisions
climb on
against that rare face

*

Tomcats in the alley
are sometimes children crying
your dream is soundless
we climb with our backs to it
toward the top
that's not in view

*

Often I hear those cries from the alley
but not now
no nothing
not even this poem
can squander silence

*

I watch you climb on alone

FANTASY ON BLINDNESS

Descending into the cellar's night
for wine
you trusted steps as the young
trust sleep
you held the bottle
as the very old grasp
each other's hands

*

We drank
then broke the loaf
of bone
you said *these eyes*
will be sea creatures
in the next flood

Anointed with this pale
staggering light that drains the wine
your hand above the flame
sees it's gone out

*

Hearts pitch their tired hulks
at anchor

In pain's primitive tongue
commas have been
left for eyes

18

MEDITATIONS FOR THOMAS MERTON [1915-1968]

I remember you touched doors
& I didn't know
if you wanted in
or out
I just knew you were there

then afterwards I noticed
how the cautious doors
creaked at every opening

*

Here in Lograire
I gather fallen limbs
here in winter I decipher stones
& here is where you left
your calligraphy
my brother

I savor these syllables of ice

SHADOW

Sun directs you
in night's absence

Trailing me
you catch up
enter at noon

At sunset a piece of my life
is paid to the horizon

Death's weight makes us lie down in the night
We take the shadows of others to sleep

NOCTURNE

stones close their mouths
ancient legless turtles
in a circle of hard silence

they turn their backs on us
everything is drawn inward
there is some whispering
among them some whispering
without breath

CESAR VALLEJO DIED ON A RAINY NIGHT

When I died
I was walking in cold rain
I remember it well
those familiar alleys
my old shoes

When I died I was walking
drenched night alleys
dreaming her face
her placid flesh
no one else had travelled there

When I died
I remember it well
her staring eyes
smooth remote stones
underwater
alone

Dying
the sky emptied me
without regret
shoes stripped off
pockets picked
flattened as usual
over smooth stones
over dangerous waters

A STONE FROM MIGUEL HERNANDEZ

smooth stone
        patient listener
i hold silence in my palm

        i speak i can't not speak
without one murmur
you cover my grave

FORGETTING

I see a cat in moonlight
black cat in snow
he's not evil
not a mystery
not mine
I see a bone-white moon
it's not romantic
it rests at an odd angle
perhaps not an odd angle
for a moon

Cat in moonlight
black in snow
the snow must be white
the trail must be filled with moonlight
impossible to follow
I never followed
not in winter
it need not be winter
cat need not be
completely black
nothing crackled nothing froze
he always returns at dawn to be fed

Cat in moonlight
no one's cat
impossible to follow
what's left out I remember
what's put in I forget
white cat
with a white cat
all is forgiven

Impossible
impossible to see
I can't take a step
boots you must
no
impossible
impossible to stop this
I forget how it's done
I only remember I can go on for a long time
stop me
no chance to
impossible
stop me
I can forget everything

II

I sing quietly to the immediate heart
One more wild hope dies of affliction

—Thomas Merton

LA LUNA LLENA

I

you took my name
deep into the rainforest

i will always follow you
but only by night

because you are so delicate
you leave a precise trail in the snow

because you are so immense
your eyes are in every tree

your calcium light is a spine that goes on forever

II

who designed this cello
for your body
who will compose sonatas
of your thighs

who stretched these strings
to slash my tongue
who will taste these elegies
along your wrists

light
so light is my saliva
asking forgiveness
among your toes

III

at the orphanage they said: it is time

to unravel the cord
it is the same cord
only longer
it will always be the same cord
only more tangled
it will seek its two directions

this way
to the mouth of your mother
or that way
to the womb of a cat

IV

they said: do not tremble child

there is nothing to fear
by now your mother is too old
to eat her young
she devoured your brothers
but we managed to save you

you were the youngest son
perhaps she was too full to finish
perhaps you were intended for dessert
perhaps you were being set aside
for another day

V

if you had my child *luna*
i would steal his milk
if you wanted flowers lady
i would poison their pot

glass will never bend
mother
this milk is cold

sweet slivers
sink all the way down
this milk is dead

i have dispatched small animals ahead of me
with bits of my clothing
to litter your camp

VI

they said: you are on your own now

it is likely
your mother has lost her teeth
though not her charms

you will be the stronger
if you find her

she will be rotten
the smell might be too much
to lie down with

this
of course
a common dilemma
yes
your father is dead
he has always been dead

VII

and they said: the hot womb

of the cat
is the other way
she will be young
and dangerous

you will be too old
perhaps even rotting
if you find her

but you must unravel you must always unravel

the cord will lead either way
it is not for you to choose
or deny
punishment will be levied anyway

careful now
our counsel is completed

stupid child
already you have lost
your first finger

VIII

i have other fingers mother
luna
waning moon
i have more than one
for each of your teeth

i have other tongues panther
puma
seething cunt
i have more than one
for each of your ovens

IX

what are you
but some blind
          disembodied
sucked-out breast

i am finished with not being able to
have you
luna

in the morning you
are a crescent of ice
a sliver of frozen milk
a bone discarded
by the smallest creatures

last night you were bloated
this morning
borrowed light returns to the sun

X

then *luna* answered: you are

done child

you have tried to steal
what is borrowed
you have only begun to unravel what is endless
you have lost your hands

on the night of my full moon
    you will be blindfolded
        and bound
        and gagged

you will be tossed
to the indifferent waters
with heavy stones
you will finally meet your mother

XI

i looked back toward the orphanage

they said nothing
they closed the door

III

You can hold back from the suffering
of the world, you have free permission
to do so and it is in accordance with
your nature, but perhaps this very
holding back is the one suffering you
could have avoided.

—Kafka

BEGINNING WITH A LAST LINE BY REVERDY

The unheard of wound I want to cure
will know pain
but leave no scar

*

Ground swells
          refusing to open
graves have lives in them already

Everywhere rodents build mounds
too small to believe in

*

Wind
    knowing it has lost
what can never be found
enters the emptiness that's always been there
    goes mad
crushes a straw shack

THE IVORY TABLE

This typewriter
   worn ribbon
   cheap recycled paper
   antiqued table
it folds inward
leaf upon leaf upon leaf
   how to divide a table into words
the table is hers

          *

A drowning woman
       rises from the waist
with the sudden awareness that it's my weight
       and her ecstasy
into which we are sinking

          *

Face swells in the mirror
mouth a wound
suffers pink

I want to kiss hollows
along her neck
        pale flesh twitches
then angry red ropes against her back

This neck reminds me
of its coolness: hurry

My arms wrap the body
sagging under another man's
anxious seed
                but she's a patient wife
turning from the mirror from herself
to me she turns
but my eyes will not stay open
closed
close on themselves
close for not having been
the first father inside her

                        *

She glides
                down
                        away from me
into love

She's forgotten everything

I try to enter
her metaphor
but the cave's interior
recedes to its walls

Before she can tell me nothing of where she's gone
she goes on burying me
in her moist earth

                        *

Light fills up every corner at once
I move from room to room
with empty slippers

Down the stairs
no one to meet me
I leave for the last time

I see shadows taking their shapes
on the ivory table

YOU SLEPT FOR DAYS

You slept for days
after nights
of crying
doorknobs stared
ceiling looked on
dumbfounded

Outside the snow was sincere
but it was melting

*

In a dream you leaped
from our flaming tin can
          a parachute of motherhood
bruising the sea

I took it down then (stupid fingers
refused to believe sharp edges
          down then
(blinking eyes   gaping evidence
          down then
deadstick landing

*

47

All winter the boy shoveled snow
scuttled neighbor's cars
healed snowball wounds
streetkeeper
massive hydrocephalic
genius of courtesy
your eyes blink from the strain

*

Mascara smeared this morning
you might have been beaten in the night
years ago
when I would see this
I would laugh
you were my little clown

A red hair
caught in the soap's throat
rain winter's last rain
exasperatingly soft
I stare out the wide-paned window
I open it
my voice escapes into silent
photographs of air

WAKING

Magellan eyes navigated dark
I sank Atlantis inside you

After winds
we slept in the hurricane's vision

I woke treading water
then swam a vicious butterfly

here's a swimmer
already past his prime
I no longer love the water

REASONS WHY YOU'RE DEAD
AT THE END OF THESE POEMS

Pink palm against pink mouth
a forgotten fig leaf

Powdered breasts splayed
sugar in its crusted bowl

Bartered thighs on glaciers of bedsheets
I've murdered myself
inside you

Still breathing I write this down
silences between breaths are petty fears
wrists are too thin a risk

Impossible to know which stars are dead
stars that signal from memory
moon living the borrowed life

I DON'T CARE WHERE YOU GO

burnt-out fragments
meteors never find their dust
your letters legal yellow
i stuff your face
i won't go near you

tonight this tentative snow
utterly without conscience
turns itself to soot

                    *

incest made me colorblind
greens are reds
blues are shadows
incest made me
sterile
legal yellow
not my incest

you're so dramatic

yes i slash my wrists
with sticks of butter

                    *

i'm on the side of inmates
bound in cumbersome clothes
i'm on the side of the moon
dark side
craters to be named for cities
eyes gouged out
i'm on the side of weary crickets
engines eat their legs of song

i'm on the side of

    i stand stiffly
    joy is inert

your poems are chopped-up somehow

i've dreamed your freckled breasts
i ate everything in the house

o dainty testicles
effeminate in their way
they roll a ritual
in their shriveled sacs

    i stuff your fucking face
    i won't go near you

       *

i'm on the side of old men
they cry in the alley
how to console them
how to ignore them
the punks throw stones

i'm on the side of old men
grandfather scared
he wants to go home
to italy
to die
it's okay with him
dying's not frightening
he doesn't care
he wants to go
living scared here
sleeps with baseball bat
scared all the time

what happened to your serenity

once i dreamed of dwelling
under a chin
        without falling

you've given up

a mountain waits forever
to stick revenge
in the wind's eye

you're hopeless

i don't care where you go

mutilated poems

piece by piece hate devours its young

cheap fatalism

worms eat earth earth eats worms

you want too much

i never had what i had
incest made me
legal yellow
not my incest

you've never really suffered

o dainty shrewd testicles
burnt-out blame
        heavy freckled breasts
        joy is inert

just rhetoric

i'm on the dark side of old men
raw-legged crickets   poets
tomcats
moons

lost

a possible cure for cancer
would only make you greedy

words only words

let me stretch beyond reason
i'm a damp thrust of grass
i'm humble enough to bend

you never gave

i'm an open field of language
i fall to the knees of my own words

never

land scorched
there's nothing left to bomb
burnt-off sky
nothing left to give

but you loved me

why ask for fresh wounds
let me tear off old scars

loved me

at the window this tentative snow

EVOLUTION

I am like a man
with a heart in my back

I calmly walk away from my feelings

IV

When the mind's free
the body's delicate.

—Lear

SCATTERED RETURNS FROM REMOTE REGIONS

Was it Schubert who died young—perhaps
I'm thinking of Mozart
Grandmother lived a hundred years

Kierkegaard walked Copenhagen alleys
chased by urchins jeering *Either/Or   Either/Or*
Eliot went to London
Nietzsche went mad

Dear Grandmother
never read a book
nor had a thought
she just rocked and smiled and rocked
and smiled
and kept her mouth shut

MEDITATION ON MEAT

I cooked the meat too fast
but had an instant epigram: Too much flame
chars the outside
but fails to heat within

With that I had an immediate explication
this was an insight into personal relationships
perhaps even sex versus love
but isn't sex versus love paradoxical
ah a good question
I had a paradox
I had a ruined meal

MY IMAGE

Because I wasn't tall enough
my first wife left me

In my wedding tux
my shoulders seem broader
than they actually are
my second wife asked for a divorce

As yet
my third wife still ignores me
she's instructed me to lose weight
harden up
consult a sex manual
& lengthen my penis

This morning
I kidnapped a blind teenager—

     She has enormous tits!

A RITUAL OF HO-HUM

1

morning coffee: soggy grounds
accounted for

remodeling downstairs: hammers   saws
                                    screams
& dust
last week the old lady
passed on

2

afternoons the potplants
gauge sun

old cat wants to play
        dump him in a sack
        take him to the river

3

sunset
tired smoke curls
no sack
old lady last week died
almost murdered her   complained always
what a waste   bitch canned   canned bitch
carried out her trash like a saint

4

sleeptime
        cat lost
night of folds he folds & unfolds
endless fugue

sleeptime
        socks turn
turn inside
out
        still smell
        small smell
        i smile
i really love to smile
carried trash smiling
saintly smile
      bitch hated dust
              dust
remodeled
complained always
what a waste
waste of smiles
smiled always
stitched smile
smile of perfect syntax

FALLING IN WITH CATLADY

I fell in with catlady
a genuine lady
an old lady
nothing mythical
she's a refuge for kittens
real kittens
blind kittens
nothing symbolic
she begs in times square

I fell in with catlady
a refuge for eyeless kittens
scabby kittens
knotty kittens
gave her my bottom dollar
nothing much
a stolen dollar
crumpled dollar
god bless you son

I fell in with catlady
where does she find them
mucous kittens
how do they find her
they sleep with open eyes
blinking means nothing
real eyes
nothing symbolic
they tremble in times square

I fell in
catlady
she made love
god bless you son
not like an old lady
not like a lady
claws
knotty claws
eyes
bloodshot eyes
bottom dollar
nothing much
god bless you son
it was nothing
crumpled
eyes open
we ate
it was nothing
trembling
nothing
we ate
the tiniest tabbies

THE EVIL EYE

Stalking this fly I get
murmurs of approval
& awe for the cannibal

I hear high-pitched voices
I stare
he's giving us the evil eye

       Eating this fly
       I turn away
       I luxuriate on the rug
       I clean
       clean myself
       lick myself clean: front legs
       back legs
         tongue to paw
         paw to face
       I clean

When they clean yes washrag clean yes
singing in the shower clean
they clean with rags of guilt
I clean
raspy tongue to paw
paw to face
eyes closed I clean
clean for pleasure

THE BLUE DEATH WISH

Death was a Royal Lady in a long blue dress
who sat at a player-piano
loving the blues

It was my turn to turn the pages
of her azure tune
while pale fingers levitated
above my wish

It was my turn and I knew the tune
unbuttoning button after cobalt button
as I went down
   I ate her moons
   I ate the shadows of her waist and thighs
my turn
to turn sapphire strands
around my tongue
my turn
to powder hairs with arsenic
my turn and I knew the tune
of turning her night of folds
into my appetite
my turn
to know until the tune was done
my turn to die inside her scimitars

JUST ONE OF MY AESTHETIC PROBLEMS

Ah these poems about sucking
    eating
            devouring
death
it's a weakness
I hate weakness
I hate weak people
        except myself
        except my weakness
it's a weakness
I love my weakness
love makes me weak
        needing strength
I devour everything
I eat to strengthen my poems
I suck what's inedible
death sucks the rest

REFRAIN

Once the fire breaks out
        I go singlefile
                off the one-step fire escape

        Falling
        I count
      the flames on my toes

        If there's ten
I return

FOOTNOTES FOR THIS TEXT ON METHOD ACTING

1 a) wound or no wound*
    wrap a soiled bandage
    around skull

  b) do not remove

---

* encourage infection

V

AT A TURN IN THE RIVER

Fish are lifted
by slow currents
from the bottom up

A boat dips then rises out of water

The angle of a fishing pole
alters without notice

Far below crabs scuttle
deeper in sand

THE LAST DECADE

Moonface
    odd-angled delicacy
eyes a pale blue notion
sockets thumbed with the doughy scar tissue
of no-contest

Torso coat-hangered
voice the cadence of thin lips
of halt   of breathlessness
laughter the genius of last-chance

Hands
    hands wrestling
  with noxious air
    hands
anxious hands
angel of death hands

TESTING ASTRONAUTS

my heart has been sucked out

      of its smug corner   orbits

          chambers falling

away

      in obsolete stages

i keep my hand over the hole in my chest

        lungs leaping

salmon upstream

THE HELICOPTER

Knowing this sound can lay on them
death
   they crouch
waiting for the chopper
to bend its flaps

The soldier's face is more
than apprehensive
more than black
his weapon juts out in four directions

The whirring ceases
they watch the back
of the soldier's neck
bent
they are tired
dust is in their eyes
teeth have aged

All around them
the entire landscape defined
by it: debris

Once in another language
it was called a village

THE PRISONER IS PUSHED INTO QUICKSAND

Shoulder blades are no match for bayonets
I thrash
    then halt
spreading calm arms

An empty bottle misses my skull
can't sink to where my thighs have gone

When her mouth reaches my heart I begin
to love my shoulders as never before
they are the last mountains
before the last desert
I will see

My chin becomes a shelf on the sand

Once she has swallowed their victim
she has swallowed their power—see how simply
my enemies have been killed

I never knew my lover until now

A DREAM OF HIROSHIMA

it dropped off

a leaf

floating

camouflaged sky

i could almost reach down   touch it

then it was gone

inside itself

we turned away toward home

stateside i went crazy
     with booze
     & broads
     & petty thefts

nights have lasted longer than i expected
this life of mine
this slow fuse

DYING

skeletons levitate
            above
    their fallen flesh

then rise as one luminous arc
        a bleached crescent on the horizon

lastly
   this scythe judging wheat
      prepares carcasses for the earth

THERE ARE IMPURITIES IN MY FUGUE

1

Ice is the final decision
temperature's idea

mice in walls
backs crackling
in windows stiff dogs die

2

Spring nudges
there's nothing to be said
for spring

Father, you write such kind letters
you've become a good son to me

3

Enemy eyes
padded warm with fat
slant against the snow

I light a match
we're not allowed to light matches
it ignites the sea

4

I grin at winter's glacial conscience
our enemy is short

I light a match
his women are tiny

Rasputin's shank is tossed
in the hay

5

Tedious inertia: sultry mice drag

I need an expert   any expert
I scrape pantry shit

Smug clock
its hands are clasped
I grin my grin Father
I scratch my match Mother

Summer is a bitch in heat

6

Your letters: *can't find*

Telegram: OFFICIAL

Darkness is   nothing is
more humble than absence

Enemy eyes have burnt out

VI

ARS POETICA

The tired horse pulls up short
   he's never been a galloping horse
   might've been a trotter with stiff reins
   perhaps even a mule

The old horse has blinders
   blinders are permitted
   nothing reprehensible
   blinders are for jumping
this horse needs courage not more style

He pulls up at the cliff's edge
it is winter
he breathes heavily
his breath travels on alone out over the valley

THREE SELF-PORTRAITS

Matisse

in this corner my tongue
holds back the scarlet walls

      a monkey examines my fossilized brain
      an open window is my pancreas escaping

at the bottom eyes float their fish
i am hardly in this painting at all

Braque

_____

my nose is a short ski slope

    here scream my ears
    under a flattened cigarette pouch

my teeth are a row of days a discarded
calendar: s m t w t f s : just like that

in other cubes it's rumored
the rest of me is hiding

Klee _____

```
i                                      sometimes
am                                     i paint
the                                    as a child caught
thin     might have my economy        or a matchstick
stick                swept away        lost
figure   by any anonymous wind         in this blizzard
drawn              but                 of white
fast          as with you                and time
and      he hesitates                  a canvas
so           and looks again                so
i                                                   i
```

VAN GOGH'S BEDROOM AT ARLES

morning leans on the walls
the walls lean on the bed
this room moving as a boxcar moves
smuggled by some train

his originals hang in this original
old clothes hanging   a tawdry towel hanging
by a nail

two chairs of wood / straw
balance
on the upturned floor

vincent outside the canvas
of the painting of the room
time a transparent flora opening

smell it as you think it speeds past

A CLASSICAL SONATA

Allegro

A long lean uncertain curve of thigh
is reluctant
    a fog that tunes up
    but will not play

I want to say flesh forgets its theme
but this is to be cheerful
cheerful and fast

Andante

Walking slowly walking
down a path
you know well enough to walk slowly down
flesh curves out again

Sadness is remote
a rumor of footsteps gone on ahead of you
steps you must live up to
or rub away

Minuet

Assuming we're assuming nothing
as we might assume the sea assumes nothing
when it turns toward a dumbfounded shore
for form
        let us assume a dance
        a dance in which your limbs

are parenthetical
a dance you will miss as a dance is missed
by the limbs later

Presto

In that classical dream you are running running
but getting no place

They are after you
they are gaining on you
and in that instant just before the first assault
of hands: you stop

DELIVERED TO AN IMAGINARY BROTHERHOOD

We will accuse each other of too much Romanticism
or half-assed truths or outright lies
we will never agree on a Manifesto

Ah but it's fine to think about
a Brotherhood without firearms or agenda
a Brotherhood without words
without each other
if that was necessary

I see this suggestion comes just at the wrong time
there are footprints on her skull
the moon is not a lady anymore

I mean a Brotherhood of some shape
I know we can't agree
I can understand that
but perhaps
why not
oh yes I see
on most nights you can't tell
Venus from Mars

BAGATELLES

Call me Isla
or Bonazzi
or I might be *tiempo*
where weather
& time
are one word

that's where I went looking for this scrap
of flesh that once joined twins
a bottle in search of a note
a tongue of water after harsh tobacco
I count my beads lightly one *luna*
two *domingo*   three *bagatella*   four *nada*
not one word more an hour not one word
can sustain
nothing

this paper is unlined
I'm sliding into these empty open pews
mis ojos son gatos
my fingers are smoking
not one word more *no más palabras*

the inversion of the exotic
is exotic

THE LATEST DOCUMENTATIONS
BEFORE ADMITTING DEFEAT

A. Your voice of long-distance tunnels my sleep

B. I want to believe the moon's Romantic
    yet she's littered with sailor's teeth

C. Fighting you again it's dreams
    of gripped hands

D. You said *I'm in the homestretch
        of my pre-existence
        & all bets are off*

XXX. I've written three poems that lost faith
    in the final turn

Y. Scars are no wiser than wounds

Z. Voice last night undoing this poem

INSOMNIA

You float effortlessly on a missing raft
you're the genius of another country

I wait with tired plants folded
sultry cats curled
I could slip out every night

there's no place I want to go